Drones

Teaching Tips

Orange Level 6
This book focuses on the phoneme **/o_e/**.

Before Reading
- Discuss the title. Ask readers what they think the book will be about. Have them briefly explain why.
- Ask readers to name the missing letter for each word on page 3. What do they notice about the "o" sound in these words? Is the "o" a long or short vowel in each?

Read the Book
- Encourage readers to break down unfamiliar words into units of sound. Then, ask them to string the sounds together to create the words.
- Urge readers to point out when the focused phonics phoneme appears in the text.

After Reading
- Encourage children to reread the book independently or with a friend.
- Ask readers to name other words with the /o_e/ phoneme. On a separate sheet of paper, have them write the words.

© 2024 Booklife Publishing
This edition is published by arrangement with Booklife Publishing.

North American adaptations © 2024 Jump!
5357 Penn Avenue South
Minneapolis, MN 55419
www.jumplibrary.com

Decodables by Jump! are published by Jump! Library.
All rights reserved. No part of this book may be reproduced in any form without written permission from the publisher.

Library of Congress Cataloging-in-Publication Data is available at www.loc.gov or upon request from the publisher.

ISBN: 979-8-88524-754-2 (hardcover)
ISBN: 979-8-88524-755-9 (paperback)
ISBN: 979-8-88524-756-6 (ebook)

Photo Credits
Images are courtesy of Shutterstock.com. With thanks to Getty Images, Thinkstock Photo and iStockphoto. Cover – p2–3 – Ruslan Kerimov, Alexander UruZ, guteksk7, Hurst Photo. p4–5 –photolinc, Den Rozhnovsky, p6–7 – IMVISUALS, Ivan Kovbasniuk. p8–9 – Kiterin, Myriam B. p10–11 – LALS STOCK, denis kalinichenko. p12–13 – humphery, p14–15 –Monkey Business Images, Khairil Ajhar Jaafar. p16 – Shutterstock.

Fill in the missing letter for each word.

glo_e

ro_e

pho_e

ho_e

Have you ever seen a drone zoom around high up in the air? What are drones, and what are they for?

Drones do not have people on them. They can be big or little and go high up in the air.

A remote sends a code to the drone. The remote can tell the drone to go up, down, left, and right.

Remote

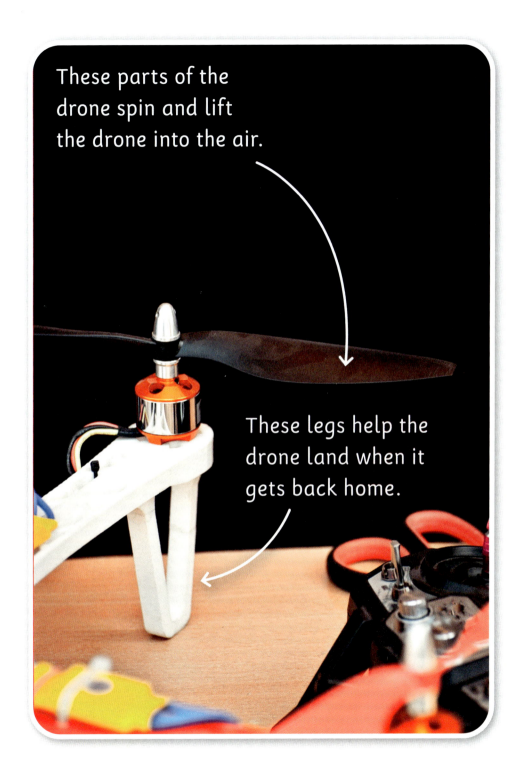

These parts of the drone spin and lift the drone into the air.

These legs help the drone land when it gets back home.

Lots of people play with drones for fun. Some drones are little and can buzz around at home.

Lots of drones are made to be outside. Some drones need a remote, and some drones need a phone.

Drones can film things from high up. They can film things with a lens as they travel.

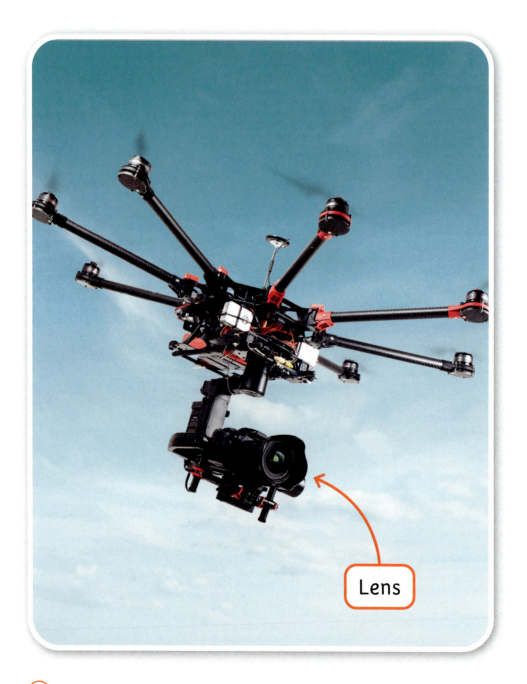

Lens

A drone can be sent high up to film some of the highest points across the globe with its lens.

Lots of drones can be sent a code that tells them to light up and get into a shape.

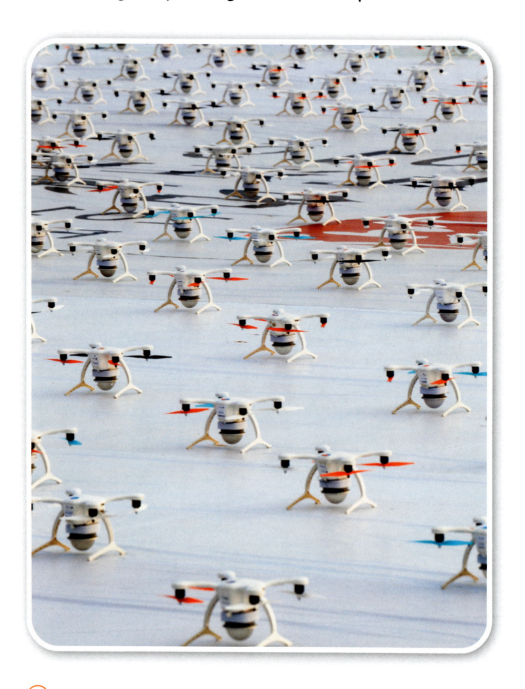

You might see a cool light display at night that has been made with drones.

If you had a drone with a lens, what might you film? Tell a teacher what you chose.

If you had 100 drones with lights, what shape might you make? What about a big rose?

Point to the objects that have /o_e/ in their name.